Now I Know

Animals at Night

by MELVIN AND GILDA BERGER

SCHOLASTIC INC.

New York Toronto London Auckland Sydney
Mexico City New Delhi Hong Kong Buenos Aires

Cover: © Manfred Danegger / Peter Arnold, Inc.; page 1: © Phil A. Dotson / Photo Researchers, Inc.; page 3: © Tui De Roy / Minden Pictures; page 4: © Royalty-Free / Corbis; page 5: © J. Allan Hobson / Photo Researchers, Inc.; page 6: © Michael Sewell / Peter Arnold, Inc.; page 7: © Erwin and Peggy Bauer / Bruce Coleman Inc.; page 8: © Shin Yoshin / Minden Pictures; page 9: © Lynda Richardson / Peter Arnold, Inc.; page 10: © Michael Quinton / Minden Pictures, small: © W. Perry Conway / Corbis; page 11: © Kim Heacox / Peter Arnold, Inc.; page 12: © Steve Maslowski / Photo Researchers, Inc.; page 13: © Konrad Wothe / Minden Pictures, small: © Joe McDonald / Corbis; page 14: © John Cancalosi / Peter Arnold, Inc.; page 15: © Michael Durham / Minden Pictures, small: © Darwin Dale / Photo Researchers, Inc.; page 16: © Michael Durham/ Minden Pictures; page 17: © Frans Lanting / Minden Pictures, small: © Ingo Arndt / Foto Natura / Minden Pictures; page 18: © Michael Durham / Minden Pictures; page 19: © Julia Sims / Peter Arnold, Inc.; page 20: © Patricia Caulfield / Peter Arnold, Inc.; page 21: © Michael & Patricia Fogden / Minden Pictures; page 22: © Image Source / Picture Quest; page 23: © Joe McDonald / www.bciusa.com; page 24: © Gabriela Staebler / zefa / Corbis; page 25: © Hugo Wilcox / Foto Natura / Minden Pictures; page 26: © Mark Boulton / Photo Researchers, Inc.; page 27: © Michael Durham / Minden Pictures; page 28: © S. J. Krasemann / Peter Arnold, Inc.; page 29: © Lynda Richardson / Peter Arnold, Inc.; page 30: © B. G. Thomson / Photo Researchers, Inc.; page 31: © Randy Faris / Corbis; page 32: © E & P Bauer / Bruce Coleman Inc.

ISBN 0-439-88848-4

18 14 15/0

Printed in the U.S.A.
First Printing, September 2006
Book design by Nancy Sabato

The sun is going down.

Night is coming.

Out goes the light.
Good night!

Hey! Who is there?

The night animals are there.
They are just waking up.

They start to look for food.

They try to keep safe.

Who is in the tree?

DID YOU KNOW?

Their large eyes help owls see in the dark.

Those large eyes belong to the owl.

What else is in the tree?
Look there.

The opossum is hanging
from the branch by its tail.

DID YOU KNOW?

Opossums eat fruit, worms, insects, and flowers.

This Australian pygmy opossum is having something to eat.

In the summer,
fireflies fill the night air.

Whoosh! What's that?

There goes a bat.

DID YOU KNOW?

Most bats eat insects that fly at night.

Bats are good fliers.
They catch and eat their dinner in the air!

Who is there?
Dark eyes are looking out
into the night.

It's a raccoon!

DID YOU KNOW?
Raccoons sleep in hollow trees.

Raccoons eat many kinds of food — even garbage!

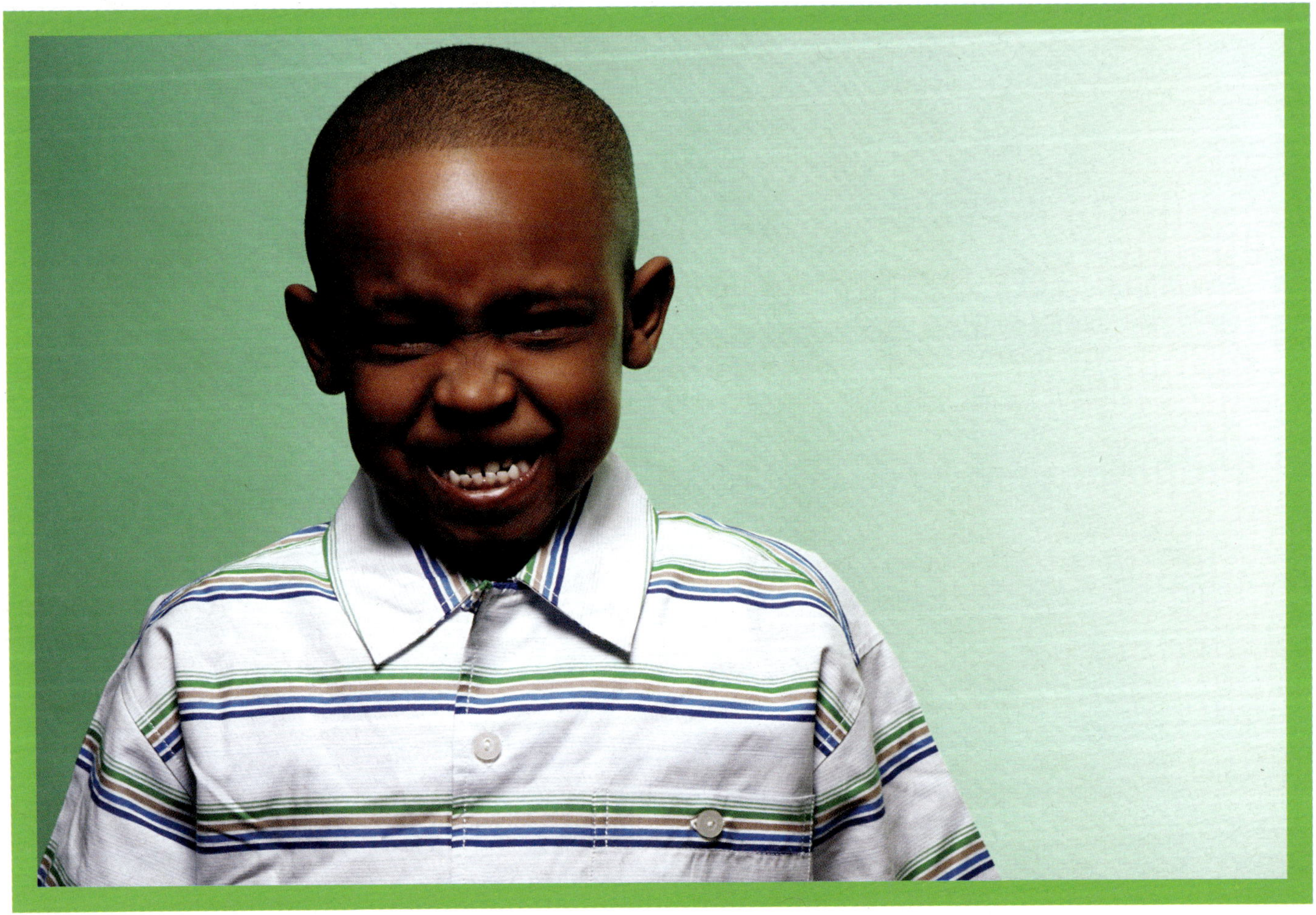

What is that bad smell?

DID YOU KNOW?

A frightened skunk lifts its tail and shoots out a smelly spray.

It's a skunk!

Let's go down to the pond.

Croak! That big noise is coming from this little animal.

It's a bullfrog.
It puffs up its neck like a balloon.

Splash!

A beaver is going for a swim.

Beavers are good swimmers.

Tonight, they are making a new home.
They build it from trees and mud.

The sun is rising.
The night animals are going to sleep.

But you are waking up.
Good morning!

GLOSSARY

Bat: A small, flying night animal. A bat is not a bird.

Beaver: An animal with a big, flat tail that lives on land or water. Beavers gnaw down trees to build their homes.

Bullfrog: A large frog with a loud, deep croak.

Firefly: A small insect that flies at night. Fireflies give off flashes of light from their bodies.

Insect: A small animal with six legs, one or two pairs of wings, and three parts to its body.

Night animal: An animal that mostly feeds by night and sleeps by day.

Opossum: A small, gray, furry night animal that lives mostly in trees.

Owl: A bird with a round head and large eyes. Owls hunt for food by night.

Raccoon: A night animal with a black-and-white face. A raccoon looks like it is wearing a mask.

Skunk: A black-and-white night animal with a bushy tail. It uses a bad-smelling spray to fight off enemies.